15 Short Stories About CATS IN EASY ENGLISH

Jenny Goldmann

BELLANOVA

MELBOURNE · SOFIA · BERLIN

15 Short Stories About Cats

in Easy English

www.bellanovabooks.com

Copyright © 2026 by Jenny Kellett

ISBN: 978-619-264-082-8
Imprint: Bellanova Books

All rights reserved. No part of this book may be reproduced in any form by any electronic or mechanical means including photocopying, recording, or information storage and retrieval without permission in writing from the author.

CONTENTS

Introduction	4
Lily's Trip to the Beach	6
Nelly Learns Her Lesson	14
Larry Hits the Jackpot	26
The Haunted House	34
The Unlikely Friendship	44
Lulu Flies Away	54
Fluffy the Diva	63
A Lucky Escape	72
The Cat Next Door	82
A Galactic Adventure	92
Mr. Whiskers and his Marvelous Mustache	100
Rascal the Cat Dog	110
No Problem Panda	118
Moggers' Special Talent	126
Rhyme's Time To Shine	134

INTRODUCTION

Welcome to "Short Stories about Cats in Easy English"! If you're a cat lover, or even just a cat admirer, this book is purr-fect for you.

Inside these pages, you'll find a collection of heartwarming, funny, and sometimes downright silly short stories all about our feline friends. From mischievous kittens to talking cats, each tale will surely put a smile on your face.

But this book is even more special because it's written in easy English. So whether you're a beginner or an advanced English learner, you can enjoy these stories without struggling to understand the language. The stories are written for learners at a B1 level. If you are an A2 level, you should still be able to understand many of the stories; just keep your dictionary handy!

And here's a tip for using this book: don't overthink it! Expect to read the stories several times before you understand them completely. Read the story through once without a dictionary and see how much you can understand. The second time, write down words you didn't know. It'll keep getting easier every time you read it!

Use the quiz at the end of each story to test your knowledge, and use the speaking/writing prompts to test yourself even further.

And finally, don't forget to take breaks to cuddle your own furry friend!

LILY'S TRIP TO THE BEACH

Lily was a beautiful fluffy white cat, with a mischievous personality. She lived with her human, a kind woman named Rachel, in a cozy little house by the sea. Rachel loved Lily more than anything, and they spent their days lounging around the house, playing with toys, and snuggling up together on the couch.

One day, Rachel decided to take Lily to the beach for a swim. Lily had never been to the beach before, and she was excited to explore all the sights and smells. As soon as Rachel set her down on the sand, Lily ran off towards the water, meowing excitedly.

Rachel followed Lily to the water's edge and watched as the cat splashed around in the shallows, chasing after seagulls and batting at the waves. Lily seemed to be having the time of her life, and Rachel couldn't help but smile at the sight of her beloved pet having so much fun.

LILY'S TRIP TO THE BEACH

As the sun began to set, Rachel decided it was time to head home. She called out to Lily, who was now waist-deep in the water, chasing after a particularly sneaky seagull. Lily didn't seem to hear Rachel's calls, however, and continued to splash and play in the water.

Rachel began to worry that Lily might get swept away by the waves, so she waded out into the water to retrieve her. But as she approached Lily, the mischievous cat suddenly darted off, darting through the waves and disappearing under the water.

Rachel panicked, calling out for Lily and frantically searching the water for any sign of her. But no matter how hard she looked, she couldn't find any trace of the missing cat.

Just when Rachel was about to give up hope, she heard a faint meowing sound coming from the direction of the shore. She turned to see Lily standing on the sand, shaking herself dry and looking rather pleased with herself.

Rachel ran over to Lily and scooped her up, hugging her tightly and showering her with kisses.

"Lily, you naughty cat! You had me so worried! I thought I'd lost you forever!"

Lily just purred and nuzzled Rachel's cheek, seeming to understand that she had caused a bit of trouble. From that day on, Rachel made sure to keep a closer eye on Lily when they went to the beach, but she couldn't stay mad at her beloved pet for long. After all, how could anyone stay mad at a cat who loved to swim as much as Lily did?

As the years went by, Lily and Rachel continued to visit the beach every summer.

Lily's love for swimming only seemed to grow, and she spent hours each day splashing around in the waves and chasing after seagulls.

One day, while they were at the beach, Rachel noticed that Lily seemed to be acting a bit strange. She kept diving under the water and then popping back up again, meowing excitedly. Rachel couldn't figure out what Lily was trying to show her, until she noticed a small, shiny object glinting in the sunlight.

Rachel waded into the water and retrieved the object, which turned out to be a beautiful golden ring. As she examined it, she realized that it was an old family heirloom that had been missing for years. She had searched high and low for it, but had never been able to find it.
As it turned out, Lily had stumbled upon the ring while swimming and had been trying

to show it to Rachel all along. Rachel was overjoyed at the discovery, and couldn't thank Lily enough for her help.

From that day on, Rachel made sure to always bring Lily with her whenever she went to the beach. She knew that her beloved cat had a special talent for finding treasure, and she couldn't wait to see what other hidden treasures they might uncover together.

As for Lily, she was just happy to be able to spend her days swimming and playing in the waves. She loved nothing more than the feeling of the cool water rushing over her fur, and the excitement of chasing after seagulls and other beach critters.

TEST YOURSELF

1. What did Lily find in the water?

    ○ A gold ring
    ○ A fish
    ○ A treasure chest

2. What is the name of Lily's human?

    ○ Matilda
    ○ Ryan
    ○ Rachel

3. Lily liked to swim.

    ○ True
    ○ False

DISCUSSION--WRITE OR SPEAK

1. Would you take your cat to the beach?

2. Have you met a cat that likes water?

3. What treasure do you think Lily will find next?

Answers:
1. A gold ring.
2. Rachel.
3. True.

NELLY LEARNS HER LESSON

Nelly was a plump, fluffy calico cat who was known for being mischievous. She lived with her loving owners, a young couple named John and Jane, on a small farm in the countryside. Nelly loved exploring the fields and woods surrounding their property, chasing after birds and rabbits, and basking in the warm sunshine.

One day, Nelly's owners were awoken early in the morning by the sound of panicked clucking coming from their chicken coop. They rushed outside to find Nelly strutting proudly around the pen, a plump and satisfied look on her face.

"Oh no, Nelly!" cried Jane, covering her mouth

in shock. "You killed one of our chickens!"

John was livid. "I can't believe it! How could you do this, Nelly? You know better than to mess with our animals!"

Nelly just looked at them with a calm, almost smug expression, as if to say, "What can I say? I'm a cat. It's in my nature."

Despite their anger, John and Jane couldn't stay mad at Nelly for long. She was just too cute, with her fluffy fur and big, bright eyes. They decided to give her a stern talking-to and let her off with a warning.

The next morning, Nelly woke up feeling rested and refreshed. She stretched, yawned, and prepared to start her day. But when she tried to let out her usual morning meow, something strange happened. Instead of a loud, cat-like mew, all that came out was a pitiful, strangled chicken noise.

"Bawk! Bawk! Bawk!" Nelly cried out, trying to get her owners' attention. But they just looked at her in confusion, not understanding what she was trying to say.

Nelly was mortified. She had always prided herself on her beautiful meow, and now it was gone! She tried again and again to make a normal cat noise, but all that came out was more bawking.

John and Jane couldn't stop laughing at the sight of their poor cat making chicken noises. They tried to talk to her, but all Nelly could do was flap her wings and squawk like a chicken.

As the days went by, Nelly became more and more frustrated with her inability to communicate. She was used to being the boss of the household, but now she couldn't even tell her owners when she wanted food or attention. She began to feel like a complete outcast.

One day, John and Jane decided to take Nelly to the vet to see if there was anything that could be done about her strange chicken-like noises. The vet examined Nelly thoroughly, but couldn't find any physical reason for her strange behavior.

"I think it's just a phase she's going through," the vet said, patting Nelly on the head. "Some cats go through strange phases, just like humans do. Just give her some time, and I'm sure she'll be back to her normal self soon."

But Nelly wasn't so sure. She was starting to wonder if she would ever be able to meow like a normal cat again. She began to feel more and more depressed, and even stopped eating her favorite treats.

Finally, one day, Nelly had had enough. She decided to take matters into her own paws and set off on a journey to find a solution to her problem. She wandered through the fields and woods, asking every animal she met if they knew of a way to fix her meow.

She asked the birds, the rabbits, and even the squirrels, but none of them had any helpful advice. Nelly was starting to lose hope when she stumbled upon a wise old owl perched in a tree.

"What seems to be the problem, my dear?" asked the owl, tilting its head to one side.

Nelly told the owl about her predicament, and the wise old bird listened patiently. After a moment of thought, the owl spoke.

"I think I may have a solution for you, Nelly," it said. "But it will require a bit of bravery and determination on your part."

Nelly's ears perked up. "Anything, I'll do it!" she exclaimed.

"Very well," said the owl. "You must journey to the top of the highest mountain in the land.

There you will find a magical spring, guarded by a powerful dragon. Drink from the spring, and your meow will be restored."

Nelly's eyes widened. "A dragon? Are you sure?"

The owl nodded. "It is the only way. Are you ready, Nelly?"

Nelly took a deep breath and nodded. "I'm ready. Thank you, wise owl. I'll do whatever it takes to get my meow back."

And with that, Nelly set off on her journey to the top of the mountain. It was a long and difficult journey, filled with challenges and obstacles, but Nelly was determined. She climbed over rocky cliffs, waded through icy streams, and braved the elements to reach her destination.

Finally, after what seemed like an eternity, Nelly reached the top of the mountain. She saw the magical spring, sparkling in the sunlight, and the scary dragon guarding it.

Nelly approached the dragon cautiously, her heart beating fast. But to her surprise, the dragon didn't attack. It looked at Nelly with kind, understanding eyes and spoke in a gentle voice.

"You have come a long way, Nelly," it said. "You are a brave and determined cat. Drink from the spring, and your meow will be restored."

Nelly didn't need to be told twice. She ran to the spring and took a long drink from the cool, clear water. And as she did, she felt a strange sensation wash over her. Her meow returned, stronger and more beautiful than ever before.

Nelly let out a joyful cry, and the dragon smiled. "I am glad to have helped," it said. "Now go, Nelly, and use your meow for good."

Nelly thanked the dragon and set off back down the mountain, her heart full of joy and her voice strong and clear. When she returned home, John and Jane were overjoyed to see her back to her normal self.

"We were so worried about you, Nelly!" cried Jane, giving her a big hug.

"We missed your beautiful meow," added John, scratching her behind the ears.

Nelly purred contentedly, happy to be home and grateful for her restored meow. And as she sat on the windowsill, basking in the warm sunlight, she made a promise to herself: she would never eat a chicken again, and she would always respect and protect the wildlife around her.

From that day on, Nelly lived a happy and peaceful life, exploring the fields and woods with a new appreciation for all the creatures that called them home—especially chickens. And even though she was still a bit mischievous at times, she knew that her actions had consequences, and she always tried to do the right thing.

TEST YOURSELF

1. What animal did Nelly eat?

   ○ A fox
   ○ A chicken
   ○ A fish

2. What animal gave Nelly helpful advice?

   ○ A squirrel
   ○ An owl
   ○ A rabbit

3. The dragon was very scary.

   ○ True
   ○ False

DISCUSSION--WRITE OR SPEAK

1. Do you think John and Jane should have been annoyed at Nelly for eating their chicken?

2. Do you think Nelly learned her lesson?

3. Why do you think people assume dragons are scary?

Answers:
1. A chicken.
2. An owl.
3. False.

LARRY HITS THE JACKPOT

Larry was a scruffy, brown cat who had grown up on the streets. He didn't have a home, and he had to fend for himself. He was always looking for something to eat, and he never had enough to eat.

One day, Larry saw a huge mansion with big, beautiful windows and a grand entrance. He had never seen anything like it before. He watched from afar and soon realized that the owners of the mansion were rarely home.

One day, when he was really hungry, Larry decided to sneak in through an open window. He was amazed by the luxurious interior of the mansion, and he couldn't believe his eyes. He went straight to the kitchen and found the fridge full of fancy food like caviar, smoked salmon, and steak.

Larry was in heaven, and he kept coming back every time the owners were out. He would eat his fill and then leave before they returned.

LARRY HITS THE JACKPOT

One day, however, Larry was caught by the owners. They were surprised to see a scruffy cat in their kitchen eating their expensive food. At first, they were angry, but then something amazing happened. The owners, who were animal lovers, were charmed by Larry's scruffy appearance and his resourcefulness. They decided to take him in as their own pet.

Larry was overjoyed. He had never had a home before, and he couldn't believe his luck. He was finally safe and loved. He no longer had to worry about finding food or a place to sleep.

The owners showered Larry with love and attention, and he soon became the king of the mansion. He had his own cozy bed, a wide variety of toys to play with, and plenty of delicious food to eat.

Larry spent his days exploring the mansion

and lounging in the sun. He would often curl up on the owners' laps and purr contentedly. Life was perfect, and Larry was the happiest cat in the world.

As time went by, Larry became more and more attached to his owners. He would follow them around the mansion, meowing for attention. He would often curl up with them in bed at night, purring softly.

One day, the owners decided to take Larry on a trip. They packed their bags and took him on a road trip to the countryside. Larry had never been on a trip before, and he was excited to explore the new surroundings.

When they arrived at their destination, Larry was amazed by the beautiful countryside. He loved the fresh air, the sunshine, and the freedom to roam. He spent his days chasing butterflies and lying in the sun.

LARRY HITS THE JACKPOT

One day, as he was exploring the countryside, Larry came across a group of cats. They were all different colors and sizes, and they were all playing together. Larry was hesitant at first, but then he decided to approach them. To his surprise, they welcomed him with open paws.

Larry was overjoyed to have made new friends. He spent the rest of the trip playing and socializing with the other cats. He had never felt so happy and content.

When they returned to the mansion, Larry was a changed cat. He was more outgoing, more confident, and more loving than ever before. He no longer just followed his owners around, but he would often wander outside to socialize with other cats.

The owners were so proud of Larry and all he had overcome. They knew that they had a very special cat, and they loved him more than ever. They continued to take him on trips to socialize with other cats. Over the years, Larry made feline friends in Paris, London, New York and beyond. Some of them even came to visit him.

So despite his poor start to life, Larry remained the happiest cat in the world.

TEST YOURSELF

1. Why was Larry so happy to find the mansion?

   ○ He was a hungry street cat
   ○ He was interested in real estate
   ○ He was cold

2. What food did Larry help himself to?

   ○ Sweetcorn, avocados and rice
   ○ Cat food and cream
   ○ Caviar, smoked salmon and steak

3. Larry went back to living on the streets.

   ○ True
   ○ False

DISCUSSION--WRITE OR SPEAK

1. Would you take in a street cat if it snuck into your house?

2. Do you think that Larry's humans should adopt another cat? Why?

3. Would you like to live in a mansion with unlimited food?

Answers:
1. He was a hungry street cat.
2. Caviar, smoked salmon and steak.
3. False.

THE HAUNTED HOUSE

Once upon a time, in a small town, there lived a group of cats who were the best of friends. They did everything together, from playing with yarn to catching mice. But one day, they decided to do something different: explore the haunted house across the street.

No other cats had ever gone in there before. It was an old, abandoned mansion that had been standing for years. People said that it was haunted, and that strange things happened inside. But the cats didn't believe it. They wanted to solve the mystery of whether or not it was really haunted.

The group had four cats: Tiger, Luna, Midnight and Whiskers. They started walking towards the mansion, their tails swaying back and forth with excitement. As they walked towards the mansion, Tiger, the bravest of them all, took the lead. He had always been fascinated by the mansion and was determined to solve the mystery of the haunted house.

THE HAUNTED HOUSE

As they approached the haunted mansion, the cats saw that it was as spooky as they had imagined. The windows were broken, the doors were creaking, and the garden was overgrown. But they didn't let that stop them. They bravely walked inside, their hearts beating fast.

As soon as they entered the mansion, something very scary happened. The doors slammed shut behind them, and the cats were trapped inside. They meowed for help, but no one heard them.

Suddenly, they heard strange noises coming from upstairs. It sounded like something was moving around. The cats were terrified, but they couldn't resist their curiosity. They decided to investigate.

As they crept up the stairs, they saw that the hallway was covered in cobwebs. The walls were peeling, and the floorboards creaked with every step they took. Suddenly, the cats heard a loud banging noise, and they jumped in fright.

Tiger was the first to investigate. He walked towards the room where the noise was coming from. When he opened the door, he saw a ball of yarn rolling across the floor, as if someone was playing with it. But there was no one there. The other cats were shocked.

Just then, the door slammed shut behind them, and they heard a loud meow. They looked around, but they couldn't see anything. Suddenly, they saw a shadowy figure in front of them, and they could hear a faint meow. They couldn't believe it. Was it a ghost?

The shadowy figure approached them, and they saw that it was a cat ghost! He introduced himself as Snowy, and he was the ghost of a cat who had lived in the mansion a long time ago.

Snowy told them that he had been trapped in the mansion for years, and that he had never met any cats who were brave enough to come in. He was pleased that the four cats had come to visit him, and he promised to tell them lots of stories about the mansion.

As the night went on, the cats learned a lot from Snowy. He showed them secret rooms and hidden passages that they would have never found on their own. He told them stories about the people who had lived in the mansion, and about the cat who had been his best friend.

But the most exciting thing that Snowy showed them was how to become invisible!

The cats were amazed. They couldn't believe that they could become invisible. Snowy showed them how to do it, and the cats spent the rest of the night practicing.

As dawn broke, the cats were exhausted. They said goodbye to Snowy, promising to visit him again soon. As they walked out of the mansion, they felt a sense of accomplishment. They had faced their fears and had found a new friend in Snowy.

But as they were leaving, they heard a loud meow coming from inside the mansion.

They turned around and saw that the door had closed again, trapping them inside. The cats were scared, but they knew that they had to face their fears and find a way out.

They searched the mansion, looking for

THE HAUNTED HOUSE

a way out, but all the doors and windows were locked. They felt trapped, until they remembered what Snowy had taught them: how to become invisible.

The cats closed their eyes and focused. They felt a strange sensation, as if they were disappearing. When they opened their eyes, they saw that they were completely invisible! They could walk through walls and doors without being seen.

The cats knew what they had to do. They went back to the room where they had first seen Snowy, and they saw a key on the table. They knew that it was the key to the front door, but they also saw that a big, scary dog was guarding it.

The cats didn't hesitate. They used their new-found power to sneak past the dog, grab the key, and unlock the front door. They ran out of the mansion, feeling victorious.

As they ran home, they couldn't stop talking about their adventure. They were amazed that they had found a friendly ghost, and that they had learned how to become invisible. They couldn't wait to tell their other cat friends all about it.

When they arrived home, they saw that their other cat friends were waiting for them. They told them all about their adventure, and how they had found a friendly ghost.

From that day on, the cats were known as the bravest cats in town. They had faced their fears, made a new friend, and had learned a new skill. They knew that they could do anything, as long as they stuck together and were brave.

And as for the mansion, it remained a mystery to everyone else. No one else saw the friendly ghost, or learned how to become invisible. It was the cats' little secret, and they were proud of it. They knew that they had found something special, and they would always cherish their adventure in the haunted mansion.

TEST YOURSELF

1. What was the name of the cat ghost?

    ○ Snowy
    ○ Frosty
    ○ Sneezy

2. Which cat was the bravest?

    ○ Whiskas
    ○ Tiger
    ○ Midnight

DISCUSSION--WRITE OR SPEAK

1. Would you go into a haunted house?

2. What would you do if you could be invisible?

3. What is the most scared you have ever been?

Answers:
1. Snowy.
2. Tiger.

THE UNLIKELY FRIENDSHIP

In a small house on the edge of town, lived a cat named Mittens. Mittens was a gray and white tabby who loved to take naps and play with balls of yarn. She lived with her owner, Mrs. Thompson, who doted on her and gave her plenty of treats.

One sunny day, as Mittens was lounging in the garden, she spotted a small mouse scurrying by. Mittens, being a cat, was naturally inclined to chase and capture the mouse. But as she was about to pounce, something unusual happened. The mouse stopped in its tracks and stared up at her.

"Hello there," said Mittens, puzzled. "What's your name?"

The mouse, whose name was Squeaky, was equally surprised to hear a cat talking to him. "I'm Squeaky," he replied, looking around nervously. "Are you going to eat me?"

Mittens chuckled. "No, I don't want to eat you. In fact, I think we could be friends."

Squeaky was skeptical. "But cats and mice are supposed to be enemies. You're supposed to chase and kill me."

Mittens shook her head. "I'm not like other cats. I'm looking for a new adventure, and I think you could be a great companion."

Squeaky thought about it for a moment. He had never heard of a cat befriending a mouse before, but he was curious to see where this might lead. "Okay," he said tentatively. "I'll be your friend."

THE UNLIKELY FRIENDSHIP

And so, Mittens and Squeaky became unlikely friends. They spent their days exploring the garden, playing hide and seek, and sharing scraps of food from Mrs. Thompson's kitchen. Mittens enjoyed having a new friend to play with, while Squeaky was thrilled to have a cat as his protector.

One day, as they were lounging in the sun, they heard Mrs. Thompson talking on the phone.

"I think we have a rat problem in the house," she said. "I've heard some strange noises in the walls, and I saw a rat running across the kitchen floor."

Mittens' ears perked up at the mention of rats. She knew from experience that rats were much larger and more dangerous than mice, and she couldn't let her friend Squeaky be in harm's way.

"We have to do something about those rats," said Mittens to Squeaky. "I don't want them to harm you or my owner's house."

Squeaky was worried. "But we're just a cat and a mouse. How can we stop the rats?"

Mittens thought for a moment. "We'll need to team up and use our strengths to outsmart the rats. I have a plan."

And so, Mittens and Squeaky embarked on a daring mission to rid the house of rats. Mittens used her agility and stealth to sneak up on the rats, while Squeaky used his intelligence and speed to distract them.

It was a dangerous mission, fraught with peril. The rats were numerous and cunning, and they had infested the entire house. Mittens and Squeaky had to be careful not to be seen or heard, or they could be caught by the rats.

The first rat they encountered was a large and scary creature, with sharp teeth and piercing eyes. Mittens crept up on the rat from behind, while Squeaky scurried in front of it, distracting it with his fast movements and high-pitched squeaks. The rat became so focused on chasing Squeaky that it didn't even notice Mittens creeping up behind it. With a swift pounce, Mittens tackled the rat and pushed him out the back door.

"That was amazing!" exclaimed Squeaky, admiring Mittens' bravery and skill.

But there were still many more rats to deal with, and the mission was far from over. Mittens and Squeaky continued their stealthy approach, using their teamwork to outmaneuver and outwit the rats.

As they were sneaking through the kitchen, they heard a loud noise coming from the pantry. They cautiously approached the door and peeked inside. To their surprise, they saw a group of rats feasting on a large chunk of cheese.

Mittens grinned mischievously. "I have an

idea," she whispered to Squeaky.

She carefully climbed up onto the shelf above the pantry and began to sway back and forth. The rats below became curious and looked up to see what was happening. At that moment, Mittens leaped off the shelf, knocking the cheese out of the rats' grasp and onto the floor.

The rats were in a frenzy, scrambling to get to the cheese. In the chaos, Mittens and Squeaky slipped away unnoticed.

"That was brilliant!" exclaimed Squeaky, impressed by Mittens' clever plan.

As they continued their mission, Mittens and Squeaky grew closer and more confident in their abilities. They fought bravely and tirelessly, using their unique skills to overcome the rats and keep each other safe.

Finally, after many long and perilous hours, they had cleared the house of all the rats. Mittens and Squeaky collapsed in exhaustion, but also in triumph.

"That was the greatest adventure I've ever had," said Mittens, looking at Squeaky with newfound respect.

Squeaky smiled. "I never thought I'd become friends with a cat, let alone fight rats with one."

From that day on, Mittens and Squeaky were inseparable. They continued to explore the garden and play together, but they also knew that they had each other's backs no matter what. They had defied the odds and proven that even the most unlikely of friendships could be the strongest of bonds.

TEST YOURSELF

1. Why was Squeaky surprised that Mittens spoke to him?

   ○ He had never heard a cat talk
   ○ Cats normally eat mice
   ○ He was shy

2. What was Mrs. Thompson talking about on the phone?

   ○ Rats in her house
   ○ Last night's television
   ○ A dinner party

3. Mittens and Squeaky got rid of the rats.

   ○ True
   ○ False

DISCUSSION--WRITE OR SPEAK

1. Why do you think Mittens wanted to be friends with Squeaky?

2. What is the most unlikely friendship you have encountered?

3. What is the best adventure you have been on with a friend?

Answers:
1. Cats normally eat mice.
2. Rats in her house.
3. True.

LULU FLIES AWAY

Lulu was a black and white cat who lived in a small house in the countryside. She was a happy and curious cat, but she had one fear: heights. Lulu would never climb higher than a chair or a table, and she would always shy away from any high places. Her owner, a kind woman named Sarah, would always tell her that there was nothing to be afraid of, but Lulu just couldn't help it.

One day, Sarah had to leave for a few days to attend a family wedding. She left Lulu with her friend, who lived in a tall apartment building in the city. Lulu was excited to explore a new place, but when she saw the tall building, she froze. It was so tall that it seemed to touch the clouds!

Lulu tried to be brave, but she just couldn't bring herself to climb up to the apartment. Her heart was pounding in her chest, and her paws were shaking. She knew she had to get inside the apartment, but she didn't know how.

Suddenly, a gust of wind blew by, and Lulu was lifted off the ground. She panicked and tried to grab onto something, but she was too scared to move. She closed her eyes and braced herself for the worst.

But to her surprise, Lulu wasn't falling. She was floating in mid-air, as light as a feather! She opened her eyes and looked around. She was surrounded by a group of colorful balloons that were lifting her up into the sky.

Lulu was confused and scared, but also amazed. She had never been so high up before. She looked down and saw the buildings and streets below her. It was like nothing she had ever seen before. She wasn't afraid anymore, but she also didn't know what to do.

As she floated higher and higher, Lulu saw a flock of birds flying by. They looked so free and happy, and Lulu wanted to join them.

She mustered up all her courage and tried to fly towards the birds, but the balloons were holding her back.

Lulu realized that she needed to find a way to get rid of some of the balloons if she wanted to fly freely. She tried to pop them with her claws, but they wouldn't budge. She then spotted a sharp corner on the edge of a nearby building and decided to fly towards it.

With a deep breath, Lulu launched herself towards the edge of the building, hoping to pop the balloons on the sharp corner. But as she approached, she saw a group of seagulls sitting on the edge, enjoying the view.

Lulu panicked and tried to change her direction, but it was too late. She crashed into the seagulls, and feathers flew everywhere. The seagulls were angry, and they started pecking at her fur.

LULU FLIES AWAY

Lulu tried to defend herself, but she was outnumbered. She knew she had to get out of there as fast as she could.

She clawed at the balloons, trying to release herself from their grip. Finally, one of the balloons popped, and Lulu started falling towards the ground. She was afraid she was going to get hurt, but just then, she felt a soft cushion under her paws. It was a pile of leaves that had been raked into a big pile.

Lulu was safe, but she was covered in leaves and twigs. She looked around and saw that she was in a park. She had never been to this part of the city before, but she knew she had to find her way back to the apartment. As she walked through the park, Lulu saw a group of cats playing in the distance. They looked friendly, so Lulu approached them. They welcomed her and asked her what had happened. Lulu told them the whole story,

and the cats listened with wide eyes.
After Lulu finished telling her story, the cats started to laugh. They thought it was funny that Lulu had been lifted into the sky by balloons and crashed into seagulls. Lulu felt a little embarrassed, but she couldn't help but laugh with them.

The cats then told Lulu that they knew the way back to the apartment building. They had been there before and knew the streets well. Lulu was relieved and grateful to have found new friends.

The group of cats led Lulu through the streets, and soon they arrived back at the apartment building. Lulu felt a sense of accomplishment, as she had faced her fear of heights and made new friends along the way.

When Sarah came back from the wedding, Lulu couldn't wait to tell her all about her adventure. Sarah was surprised to hear about Lulu's experience, but she was also proud of her for being brave and making new friends.

From that day on, Lulu wasn't as scared of heights anymore. She realized that sometimes unexpected things can happen, but that doesn't mean you should give up. She had faced her fear and come out on the other side, stronger and more confident than before.

And every time Lulu saw a balloon or a seagull, she would smile to herself and remember the day she flew through the sky like a bird.

TEST YOURSELF

1. Why was Lulu trying to pop some of her balloons?

   - ○ Just for fun
   - ○ To get back to the ground
   - ○ To reach the birds

2. What did Lulu's new friends think of her adventure?

   - ○ They thought it was funny
   - ○ They didn't believe her
   - ○ They were jealous

3. Lulu still had a fear of heights after her adventure.

   - ○ True
   - ○ False

DISCUSSION--WRITE OR SPEAK

1. If you could fly, where would you go?

2. Would you like to be a bird for the day? Why or why not?

3. What is your biggest fear?

Answers:
1. To reach the birds.
2. They thought it was funny.
3. True.

FLUFFY THE DIVA

Fluffy was a Sphynx cat who lived a happy life in the leafy suburbs of a big city. She was not like other cats; she was bald and had a very unique sense of style. Her love for fashion was something that set her apart from the other cats in the neighborhood. She had a vast wardrobe of clothes, ranging from coats (she had to stay warm!), dresses, hats, and even shoes. Fluffy was famous for her fabulous wardrobe and her fashion sense was known far and wide.

One day, a famous fashion designer heard about Fluffy's unique fashion sense and decided to invite her to his fashion show in the city. Fluffy was full of excitement and couldn't wait to show off her fabulous wardrobe. She spent weeks preparing for the show, trying on

different outfits, and even hiring a personal stylist.

The day of the fashion show finally arrived, and Fluffy was the star of the event. Everyone was in awe of her stunning outfits and her confidence on the runway. Fluffy even won the award for the best-dressed cat at the show. She was now a celebrity, with fans clamoring for her autograph and pictures.

As Fluffy's fame grew, so did her ego. She became more and more demanding, refusing to wear anything that wasn't designer, and demanding to be treated like a queen. She became so difficult to work with that no one wanted to collaborate with her anymore.

One day, while she was out shopping for more clothes, she got lost and found herself in an unfamiliar part of town. She wandered around for hours, trying to find her way back home, but to no avail. Exhausted and hungry, she stumbled upon a small house with a friendly family inside.

Feeling sorry for the lost and shivering Sphynx, the family took Fluffy in and gave her a warm meal. As she sat in their lap and purred contentedly, Fluffy realized that she had been so caught up in her fame and fortune that she had forgotten the importance of kindness and humility.

From that day on, Fluffy lived a more humble and content life, still wearing her fabulous clothes, but with a newfound appreciation for the simple things in life. She realized that true happiness came not from fame or fortune, but from the love and kindness of those around her.

However, Fluffy's newfound humility was put to the test when her wardrobe was stolen. She woke up one morning to find her closet empty. Panic set in as she realized that all her designer outfits were gone. She searched high and low, but they were nowhere to be found.

Desperate for help, Fluffy turned to the local detective, a retired Bloodhound named Sherlock. Sherlock had a reputation for being the best detective in the town, and Fluffy knew that he was her best hope for finding her missing clothes.

Sherlock agreed to take the case and set to work investigating. He interviewed Fluffy's friends and acquaintances, combed the neighborhood for clues, and even went undercover in the local black market to see if he could find any leads. It was a difficult case, and he was beginning to lose hope.

Just when he was about to give up, a new clue emerged. A suspicious-looking alley cat was seen wearing one of Fluffy's stolen outfits. Sherlock quickly tracked down the alley cat, who confessed to stealing Fluffy's clothes and selling them on the black market.

With the thief caught, Fluffy was finally able to get her clothes back. However, her experience had taught her a valuable lesson.

She realized that while she loved her fabulous wardrobe, there were more important things in life, like friendship, kindness, and helping those in need.

From that day on, Fluffy used her fame to inspire others, not just with her fashion sense, but with her acts of kindness. She started volunteering at the local animal shelter, helping to find homes for cats in need. She also used her social media platforms to spread awareness about the importance of adopting pets and supporting animal rescue organizations.

Her selfless acts of kindness did not go unnoticed, and soon, Fluffy's popularity reached new heights. She was featured in several newspapers and magazines, and her fashion sense became even more popular among her fans. But what was more important to her than anything else was the joy she felt from giving back to her community.

Years went by, and Fluffy grew old. She retired from her fashion career but continued to inspire others with her kindness and generosity. When she passed away, the whole town mourned her loss, and her legacy lived on.

Her wardrobe was donated to the local animal shelter, where it was used to dress up cats who were waiting for their forever homes. Her memory became a symbol of kindness and compassion, and every year, the town held a fashion show in her honor to celebrate her life.

Fluffy's life had been full of twists and turns, but she had found her true calling, not just as a fashion icon but as a champion for the animals in her community. And that was what made her truly unforgettable.

TEST YOURSELF

1. Who was Sherlock?

    ○ The detective
    ○ Fluffy's best friend
    ○ Fluffy's owner

2. What award did Fluffy win at the fashion show?

    ○ Most fashionable
    ○ Best dressed cat
    ○ An MBE

3. Fluffy's owners stole her clothes.

    ○ True
    ○ False

DISCUSSION--WRITE OR SPEAK

1. Have you taken part in any volunteer work? If not, what would you like to do?

2. What do you think the moral of Fluffy's story is?

3. Are you interested in fashion? Why or why not?

Answers:
1. The detective.
2. Best dressed cat.
3. False.

A LUCKY ESCAPE

Once upon a time, there was a curious girl named Bella and her black cat, Lucky. They lived in a tiny village where nothing ever happened, but that all changed one dark and stormy night.

Bella and Lucky were snuggled up in bed when they heard a strange noise coming from outside. They crept to the window to investigate, and there they saw a mysterious figure lurking in the shadows. The figure was dressed in all black, with a wide-brimmed hat and a long coat that flapped in the wind.

Bella was intrigued and decided to investigate further. She quickly put on her raincoat and

boots, grabbed a flashlight, and set out into the stormy night with Lucky by her side.

As they roamed the deserted streets, they noticed that every streetlight had been switched, and there was a sense of fear in the air. Suddenly, they heard a loud crash coming

A LUCKY ESCAPE

from the direction of the old abandoned mansion on the edge of town.

Bella and Lucky bravely made their way towards the mansion, where they found that the front door had been smashed open. They crept inside and discovered that the mansion was full of strange and eerie artifacts.

As they explored the dark corridors, they came across a room with a large safe. Bella's curiosity got the best of her, and she tried to open the safe. After trying several combinations, the safe finally opened with a loud creak, revealing a mysterious object that glowed in the dark.

Just as Bella was about to examine the object more closely, she heard a noise coming from down the hallway. She quickly hid the object in her bag and, with Lucky by her side, she crept down the hallway to investigate.

What they found was a chilling surprise: the mysterious figure they had seen earlier was standing in front of them, holding a knife and looking menacingly in their direction.

Bella and Lucky were frozen with fear, but the figure didn't make a move. Instead, it just stood there, staring at them with its piercing gaze. Suddenly, it turned around and disappeared into the shadows, leaving Bella and Lucky shaken and bewildered.

Bella knew that something wasn't right, and she was determined to uncover the truth. She spent the next few days researching the mysterious object she had found in the safe and discovered that it was a powerful, magical stone that had been lost for centuries.

A LUCKY ESCAPE

Meanwhile, strange things were happening in the town. More and more people were reporting strange figures lurking in the shadows, and there were rumors of a mysterious group that was up to no good.

Bella knew that she had stumbled upon something dark and mysterious, and she vowed to get to the bottom of it. She enlisted the help of her friends, and Lucky's brave cat friends, and together, they set out to investigate.

As they roamed the town, they encountered more and more strange figures, but they managed to avoid them and continue their search. Finally, they discovered a secret room where they found a group of people dressed in black who were trying to get their hands on the stone.

Bella and her friends knew that they had to act fast, so they came up with a plan to retrieve the stone and stop the mysterious group from doing harm. It was a dangerous mission, but they were determined to succeed.

They snuck into the secret room and were met with resistance at every turn. But they managed to fight their way through and finally found the magical stone, guarded by the mysterious group leader himself.

A fierce battle took place, but Lucky and her friends fought off the enemy with their sharp claws and laser-fast moves. They had saved the town from the mysterious group and had returned the stone to its rightful place.

Bella and Lucky returned home, exhausted but happy that they had solved the mystery.

However, they still had some unanswered questions. Who was the mysterious group, and what were they trying to do with the stone?

Bella and her friends continued to investigate and finally discovered the truth. The group was made up of thieves who wanted to use the magical stone to gain wealth and power. The stone had the power to control people's minds and make them do whatever they wanted, and the group planned to use it to their advantage.

Bella and her friends knew they had to stop the group for good, so they reported their findings to the authorities. With the help of the police, the group was finally brought to justice, and the town was once again safe.

Bella and Lucky were hailed as heroes, and the town threw a big celebration in their honor.

They had solved the mystery and saved the town from danger.

From that day on, Bella and Lucky became known as the brave duo who always stood up for what was right. They continued to have many more exciting adventures, but none were as mysterious and thrilling as the one where they uncovered the dark secrets of their town.

A LUCKY ESCAPE

TEST YOURSELF

1. Where do Bella and Lucky live?

   ○ In the suburbs
   ○ In a large city
   ○ In a tiny village

2. What was the dark shadowy figure wearing on his head?

   ○ A wide-brimmed hat
   ○ A sombrero
   ○ A long coat

3. Bella and Lucky weren't able to rescue the stone, so they had to call the police.

   ○ True
   ○ False

DISCUSSION--WRITE OR SPEAK

1. Do you think your town has any dark secrets? Use your imagination!

2. Would you have gone into the scary mansion?

3. What is the weirdest thing you've seen in your town?

Answers:
1. In a tiny village.
2. A wide-brimmed hat.
3. False.

THE CAT NEXT DOOR

In a cozy little neighborhood, there lived two cats: Tom and Molly. They were next-door neighbors, but they had never met. Tom was a handsome tabby cat with bright green eyes, and Molly was a fluffy white cat with big blue eyes.

One sunny morning, Tom woke up early and decided to take a stroll around the block. As he walked by the fence that separated his yard from Molly's, he heard a faint meowing sound. He peered through the slats and saw a glimpse of white fur. Curious, he climbed up the fence to get a better look.

To his surprise, he found Molly stuck in a tree!

She had climbed up the tree to catch a bird and had gotten her paw caught in a branch. Tom quickly came to her rescue, and with a little bit of effort, he freed her from the tree. Molly was grateful and relieved, and from that moment on, the two cats became the best of friends.

THE CAT NEXT DOOR

They spent every day together, playing games and sharing treats. They chased butterflies and birds, and they even went on little adventures around the neighborhood. Their owners, who were also good friends, loved to watch the two cats have fun and play together.

One day, while they were playing, they heard a loud meowing sound coming from a nearby alley. They ran to investigate and found a little kitten who was lost and scared. Tom and Molly knew they had to help the kitten, so they brought her back to their yard and fed her some milk.

The kitten, who they named "Po," was grateful for their help and quickly became friends with Tom and Molly. They showed her the ropes and introduced her to all of their other animal friends in the neighborhood. Po was thrilled to have found such great friends.

But one day, Tom had to leave town for a week to visit his cousin. Molly was sad to see him go, but she promised to keep herself busy while he was away. Little did she know that Tom had a surprise for her when he returned.

Upon his arrival, he brought with him a beautiful collar that he had made himself. The collar was made of colorful beads, and it sparkled in the sunlight. He presented it to Molly, who was overjoyed and couldn't stop purring with happiness.

As the weeks went by, Tom and Molly continued to have fun and make new memories. They even had a big party with all of their neighborhood friends, and everyone danced and played games together. But little did they know, a big storm was headed their way.

One day, while they were playing outside,

they heard a loud rumbling sound coming from the sky. They looked up and saw dark clouds gathering above. Before they knew it, a massive thunderstorm hit the neighborhood.

The wind was howling, and the rain was pouring down. Tom and Molly were scared and didn't know what to do. But then they remembered their friend Po, who was still just a kitten. They quickly ran to her house to make sure she was safe.

To their relief, Po was okay, but her owners had left her outside in the storm. Tom and Molly knew they had to help her, so they brought her back to their yard and huddled together for warmth. They were scared, but they felt safe together.

As the storm passed, Tom and Molly realized something. They realized that they were not just best friends but that they also had romantic feelings for each other. So, they decided to become a couple.

From then on, Tom and Molly spent every day together, cuddling and napping in the sun. They were the happiest cats in the neighborhood, and their love for each other only grew stronger with each passing day. They did everything together, from playing in the yard to snuggling up for naps. They were inseparable.

But one day, a new cat moved into the neighborhood. His name was Max, and he was a big, black cat with piercing yellow eyes. He was a charmer, and all the cats in the neighborhood, except for Tom and Molly, thought he was amazing.

Max began to come around more often, and he tried to win Molly's heart. He brought her flowers and treats, but she wasn't interested.

She only had eyes for Tom.

This made Max angry, and he began to plot against Tom. He would sneak into Tom's yard and try to cause trouble, but Tom was always one step ahead. He knew what Max was up to, and he wouldn't let him get away with it.

One day, when Tom was out of town, Max made his move. He snuck into Molly's yard and tried to get her to leave with him. Molly refused, but Max wasn't taking no for an answer.

He began to chase Molly around the yard, but just as he was about to catch her, Tom returned home. He saw what was happening and knew he had to act fast.

Tom pounced on Max, and the two cats began to fight. It was a fierce battle, but in the end,

Tom emerged victorious. Max was left to lick his wounds and slink away, defeated.

Molly was relieved and grateful that Tom had come to her rescue. She realized how much she loved him and how lucky she was to have him by her side.

From then on, Tom and Molly's love grew even stronger. They knew that no matter what challenges they might face, they would always have each other—and little Po. They lived happily ever after, cuddling and playing together, and never forgetting the power of true love.

TEST YOURSELF

1. Who is Po?

    ○ A puppy
    ○ A kitten
    ○ A human

2. Why was Molly so happy when Tom returned from his trip?

    ○ He brought her a beautiful collar
    ○ He took her out for dinner
    ○ He had a haircut

3. Molly thought Max was an interesting and charming cat.

    ○ True
    ○ False

DISCUSSION--WRITE OR SPEAK

1. How well do you know your neighbors?

2. What type of weather do you get where you live? Do you have big storms?

3. What memories do you have of your first best friend?

Answers:
1. A kitten.
2. He brought her a beautiful collar.
3. False.

A GALACTIC ADVENTURE

It's the year 2056, and humans have finally colonized Mars. They built a beautiful settlement and started farming to sustain themselves. But, little did they know, they were not alone on the planet.

A group of adventurous cats had made their way to Mars, too. These felines were no ordinary cats - they had been specially trained for space travel and had survived the long journey to the red planet. They were now living happily in a cozy corner of the Martian settlement.

The cats were thrilled to explore their new home. They ran, jumped and played in the low

gravity. They were amazed by the beautiful landscapes and the stunning views of the planet. Life was purr-fect.

But, one day, something strange happened. The food supplies of the settlement started disappearing. The humans were puzzled as to what was happening. They thought it was some technical glitch in the system, but the problem continued to happen.

The cats, being the curious creatures they are, decided to investigate the matter. They soon discovered that a group of space mice had infiltrated the settlement and were stealing the food supplies. The mice were too fast for the humans to catch, but the cats were determined to stop them.

The cats came up with a plan. They gathered all the string, cardboard boxes and other items they could find to create a maze around the food storage area. They then hid and waited for the mice to come. And come, they did!

The mice scurried into the maze, but they were quickly lost. They ran into dead ends, bumped into walls and got tangled up in the string. The cats pounced on them and soon had them under control.

The humans were amazed at what the cats had accomplished. They were grateful for their furry friends' bravery and intelligence. From then on, the cats became the official guardians of the settlement, making sure that no unwanted visitors could harm their new home.

However, things took a turn for the worse when a giant dust storm hit the settlement. The humans had to take shelter inside their homes, but the cats were trapped outside. The strong winds and flying debris were too dangerous for them to navigate.

One brave cat named Sofia decided to take action. She used her claws to grip onto a nearby wall and slowly made her way to the shelter. The humans were surprised to see her and quickly opened the door to let her in. They were relieved to see that Sofia was safe and sound.

But, Sofia had more in store. She knew that the other cats were still outside and in danger. She meowed and purred, trying to get the humans' attention. They quickly understood her message and followed her outside. With Sofia leading the way, they found the other cats and brought them to safety.

The humans were amazed by the cats' bravery and intelligence. They realized that these furry creatures were more than just pets - they were valuable members of the community.

From then on, the cats and humans worked together to make life on Mars even better. The cats hunted for pests that threatened the crops, while the humans built better shelters for their furry friends.

Over time, the cats even learned how to communicate with a new language the humans had developed called Martianish. The language was inspired by the cats' meows and meant that everyone could finally talk to one another.

And so, the colony of cats on Mars lived happily ever after, exploring the planet, protecting their human companions, having interesting debates, and proving that anything is possible when you have a team that includes a group of brave and intelligent cats.

A GALACTIC ADVENTURE

TEST YOURSELF

1. Why didn't the humans know the cats were also on Mars?

    ○ The cats snuck onto the spaceship
    ○ The cats came separately
    ○ They were invisible

2. Why did the humans need the cats' help?

    ○ Mice were stealing their food
    ○ To cook them dinner
    ○ For cuddles

3. The cats were able to communicate with the humans using a new language.

    ○ True
    ○ False

DISCUSSION--WRITE OR SPEAK

1. Would you travel to Mars?

2. If you were going to Mars, what three items would you take with you?

3. If you could talk to cats, what would you talk about?

Answers:
1. The cats came separately.
2. Mice were stealing their food.
3. True.

MR. WHISKERS AND HIS MARVELOUS MUSTACHE

Once upon a time, in a small town nestled in the rolling hills of rural America, there lived a plucky little cat named Mr. Whiskers. Mr. Whiskers was a scrappy little feline with a big personality and an even bigger heart. He loved nothing more than lounging in the sun, chasing after birds, and snuggling up with his human companions on the couch.

One day, as Mr. Whiskers was napping on the couch, he suddenly felt a strange tingling sensation on his upper lip. When he opened his eyes, he was shocked to find that he had grown a full, luxurious mustache overnight!

At first, Mr. Whiskers was a little self-conscious about his new facial feature. He wasn't sure if it suited him, and he was worried that his friends and family might make fun of him. But as he strutted around town, he quickly discovered that his mustache was a hit! Everyone he met stopped to admire it and stroke it, and before long, Mr. Whiskers was the talk of the town.

MR. WHISKERS AND HIS MARVELOUS MUSTACHE

As Mr. Whiskers basked in the attention and adoration of his newfound fame, he began to see the benefits of his mustache. It made him look more distinguished and sophisticated, and he found that it gave him an air of mystery and intrigue. People were constantly asking him if he was a detective, or a famous actor, or even a secret agent.

One day, Mr. Whiskers received an invitation to appear on the local news. The reporters were fascinated by his mustache and wanted to interview him about it. Mr. Whiskers was thrilled at the opportunity to share his story with the world, and he eagerly accepted the invitation.

On the day of the interview, Mr. Whiskers dressed up in his finest suit and tie and made his way to the studio. When he arrived, he was greeted by a sea of flashing cameras and a horde of reporters hoping for a glimpse of him. Mr. Whiskers loved the attention and posed for photos, preening and posing for the cameras like a true star.

When the interview began, Mr. Whiskers sat down with the reporters and told them all about his mustache and how it had changed his life. He spoke about the attention and admiration it had brought him, and how it had made him feel more confident and self-assured. The reporters were fascinated by his story and asked him all sorts of questions about his grooming routine and how he kept his mustache looking so impeccable.

As the interview drew to a close, Mr. Whiskers thanked the reporters and waved goodbye to the cameras. As he left the studio, he couldn't help but feel a sense of pride and accomplishment. He had always known that he was a special cat, but now the whole world knew it too.

As Mr. Whiskers' fame grew, he started to receive invitations from all over the world. He was invited to cat shows, pet expos, and even international grooming competitions. Mr. Whiskers was thrilled at the opportunity to travel and see the world, and he eagerly accepted every invitation that came his way.

His first trip was to Paris, where he was invited to appear in a high-end fashion show. Mr. Whiskers strutted down the runway, looking every bit the suave and sophisticated feline he was. The audience went wild, and Mr. Whiskers couldn't help but feel like he was on top of the world.

From there, Mr. Whiskers went on to visit Japan, where he was a guest judge in a prestigious grooming competition. He met other cats from all over the world, and he was amazed by the incredible hairstyles and grooming techniques on display. He even picked up a few tips himself, and he started to experiment with new ways to style his mustache.

But despite all his travels and adventures, Mr. Whiskers always remained true to his small-town roots. He would send postcards and souvenirs to his friends and family back home, and he would tell them stories of his incredible adventures.

One day, as Mr. Whiskers was relaxing on the couch with his human companions, he received a special invitation in the mail. It was from the President of the United States, who had heard about Mr. Whiskers' incredible story and wanted to invite him to the White House for a special event.

Mr. Whiskers was stunned. He had never imagined that his mustache could lead him all the way to the White House! He eagerly accepted the invitation, and before he knew it, he was boarding a plane to Washington D.C.

When Mr. Whiskers arrived at the White House, he was greeted by the President and the First Lady. They both showered him with compliments and affection, marveling at the luxuriousness of his mustache. They even took him on a special tour of the White House, showing him all the incredible history and artifacts on display.

But the highlight of Mr. Whiskers' trip came at the end of the visit. The President and the First Lady presented him with a special medal, honoring him for his incredible achievements and his service to the cat community. Mr. Whiskers was overwhelmed with emotion, and he felt a deep sense of pride and gratitude for the journey his mustache had taken him on.

As Mr. Whiskers returned home to his small town, he couldn't help but reflect on his incredible adventure. He had gone from a simple house cat to a world-famous feline, all thanks to his mustache. But despite all the attention and adoration he had received, Mr. Whiskers knew that the most important thing in life was the love and companionship of his friends and family.

And so, as he lounged on the windowsill and watched the sun set over the rolling hills of rural America, Mr. Whiskers felt content and at peace. He knew that his mustache had taken him on an incredible journey, but he also knew that the most important adventures were the ones he shared with the people he loved.

TEST YOURSELF

1. What did Mr. Whiskers wear on the day of his first interview?

    ○ Nothing, he's a cat
    ○ A tracksuit
    ○ A suit and tie

2. What did the President give to Mr. Whiskers?

    ○ A medal
    ○ A tin of tuna
    ○ A cuddle

3. Mr. Whiskers was born with his moustache.

    ○ True
    ○ False

DISCUSSION--WRITE OR SPEAK

1. Would you like to suddenly become famous? If so, what for?

2. Would you like your cat to become an internet celebrity?

3. If you could meet any celebrity, dead or alive, who would it be, and what would you say to them?

Answers:
1. A suit and tie.
2. A medal.
3. False.

RASCAL THE CAT DOG

Rascal was a plump and fluffy feline with bright green eyes and a mischievous glint in his gaze. He was a curious cat and lived in the countryside where there wasn't much to do.

One day, while out exploring the neighborhood, Rascal stumbled upon a group of playful dogs chasing a ball in a park. As he watched them bounding and barking with joy, something inside of him clicked.

"I want to be a dog!" he exclaimed to himself.

And so, with that determination in mind,

Rascal set out to become the best dog he could be.

He started by practicing his bark. He tried to mimic the deep, throaty sounds the dogs made, but no matter how hard he tried, all he could manage was a pitiful meow. Undeterred, he continued to practice, convinced that he just needed a little more time to perfect his barking technique.

Next, he tried to mimic the dogs' body language. He wagged his fluffy tail and scratched at the door to be let in and out. He even tried to fetch a ball, but quickly learned that cats just aren't built for fetching.

Despite these setbacks, Rascal remained convinced that he was meant to be a dog. He began to think of himself as one and even adopted a dog-like personality. He would join the neighborhood dogs on their daily walks and would even try to join in on their playtime, much to their confusion.

One day, while out on a walk with the dogs, Rascal came across a juicy-looking bone on the side of the road. Without hesitation, he pounced on it and began to gnaw away.

The dogs looked on in shock as their feline friend chomped down on the bone.

"What are you doing, Rascal?" one of them asked.

"I'm a dog now, don't you see?" Rascal replied with a mouthful of bone.

The dogs couldn't help but laugh at their silly friend. They tried to explain to Rascal that no matter how hard he tried, he would always be a cat. But Rascal just wouldn't listen.

Eventually, the dogs decided to have a little fun with their stubborn friend. They convinced him to participate in a "dog show," where Rascal would be judged on his canine skills. Rascal was overjoyed at the opportunity to prove himself and spent the whole day practicing his tricks. He chased his tail, rolled over, and even tried to fetch a ball again (with limited success).

On the day of the dog show, the whole neighborhood turned out to watch. Rascal took to the stage with all the confidence of a seasoned pro, wagging his tail and barking (or rather, meowing) with all his might.

But as the judges began to evaluate his performance, it became clear that Rascal wasn't quite cut out for the canine life. He tripped over his own paws and couldn't seem to keep his balance. He even tried to climb a tree at one point, much to the amusement of the crowd.

Despite his valiant efforts, Rascal ended up taking last place in the dog show. But as he walked off the stage, head held high, the dogs and people in attendance couldn't help but cheer and clap for him.

In the end, Rascal learned that it's okay to be yourself and to embrace your unique talents and quirks. And while he may never be a dog, he was still the best cat he could be.

RASCAL THE CAT DOG

TEST YOURSELF

1. What was the first thing Rascal did to try and be like a dog?

   ○ Stick his tongue out
   ○ Chase the mailman
   ○ Practice his bark

2. What place did Rascal take in the dog show?

   ○ He didn't take part
   ○ Last
   ○ First

3. Rascal was good at catching a ball.

   ○ True
   ○ False

DISCUSSION--WRITE OR SPEAK

1. If you were a dog for the day, what would you do?

2. What unique talents and quirks do you have?

3. Have you ever taken part in a talent show?

Answers:
1. Practice his bark.
2. Last.
3. False.

NO PROBLEM PANDA

Life wasn't easy for Panda the cat. She was born with only three legs, which made it difficult for her to keep up with the other cats in her neighborhood. She would often sit on the side and watch them play, wishing she could join in. But one day, everything changed.

Panda was wandering through the neighborhood when she heard a loud meowing coming from a nearby alley. She followed the sound and found a small kitten stuck in a drainpipe. The kitten was crying for help, and Panda knew she had to do something.

With her three legs, Panda couldn't climb down into the drainpipe to save the kitten. She was about to give up when she remembered something her mother had told her: "Where there's a will, there's a way." Determined to rescue the kitten, Panda looked around for something she could use to help.

That's when she spotted an old broom leaning against a nearby wall. It was a long shot, but Panda had an idea. She grabbed the broom with her front paws and hopped on her hind legs, using the broom like a cane to steady herself.

It wasn't easy, but Panda managed to maneuver the broom down the narrow drainpipe until she reached the kitten. The kitten was scared and wouldn't stop crying, but Panda's kind eyes and soothing voice calmed her down.

Just as Panda was about to lift the kitten to safety, she heard a loud growl. She looked up and saw a big, mean-looking dog staring down at her from the top of the drainpipe. The dog barked and snarled, drool dripping from its teeth.

Panda knew she had to act fast. She picked up the kitten and held it close to her chest, trying to keep it calm. The dog started to climb down the drainpipe, its eyes fixed on Panda and the kitten. Panda was terrified, but she didn't give up.

With all her strength, Panda lunged at the dog, using the broom like a sword to fend it off. The dog barked and growled, but Panda was fearless. She fought with everything she had, determined to protect the kitten.

Finally, the dog backed off, realizing it was no match for Panda's bravery. Panda and the kitten emerged from the drainpipe victorious, covered in dirt and scratches, but alive and well.

Word of Panda's bravery quickly spread throughout the neighborhood, and she became a hero in the eyes of the other cats.

They welcomed her into their group, and from that day on, Panda was no longer left out of their games and adventures. She had made friends and found a place where she belonged.

Panda was overjoyed to finally be accepted by the other cats in her neighborhood. They welcomed her with open paws, and Panda couldn't believe how kind they were to her. She had always felt like an outsider, but now she had found a place where she belonged.

The other cats were fascinated by Panda's bravery and resourcefulness when she rescued the kitten from the drainpipe. They admired her for her quick thinking and for her willingness to put herself in danger to save another cat. Panda was grateful for the praise, but she knew that she had just done what anyone would do in that situation.

Over the next few weeks, Panda became close friends with a few of the other cats. She particularly enjoyed spending time with a black and white cat named Puddles. Puddles was also a bit of an outsider, as he had a crooked tail that made it difficult for him to balance. But together, Panda and Puddles found that they made a great team.

So, as it turned out, Panda's missing leg wasn't a disability after all. It was a unique trait that made her special and helped her to stand out from the crowd. Panda had discovered that her differences were what made her amazing, and that by working together with others, she could achieve anything she set her mind to.

TEST YOURSELF

1. What was Puddles disability?

    ○ She only had three legs
    ○ She had a crooked tail
    ○ She was blind

2. What did Panda use to rescue the tiny kitten?

    ○ A drainpipe
    ○ A magic wand
    ○ A broomstick

3. Panda was laughed at by the other cats after saving the kitten.

    ○ True
    ○ False

DISCUSSION--WRITE OR SPEAK

1. What is the bravest thing you have ever done?

2. What do you think Panda and Puddles' first adventure together will be?

3. What difficulty have you overcome to achieve something you wanted?

Answers:
1. A broomstick.
2. Last.
3. False.

MOGGERS' SPECIAL TALENT

There was never such a strange cat as Moggers. One day, Moggers was walking down the street, minding his own business, when he saw a group of dogs chasing a squirrel. Moggers had always been curious about squirrels, so he decided to follow them.

As he followed the dogs and the squirrel, Moggers realized that he was lost. He had no idea where he was, and he was starting to get hungry. Just then, he saw a mouse scurrying along the ground. He pounced on it and gobbled it up in one bite.

Suddenly, Moggers felt a strange sensation in his stomach. He realized that the mouse was a magic mouse, and it had given him the power to talk! Moggers was thrilled. He had always wanted to talk to the humans, but he had never been able to.

MOGGERS' SPECIAL TALENT

So, Moggers set off in search of the humans. He wandered around for hours, asking every animal he met if they knew where the humans were. He met a wise old owl who told him that the humans lived in a big building called a "library."

Moggers had never heard of a library, but he was determined to find it. He followed the directions the owl had given him and eventually came across a huge, imposing building with "Library" written on the front.

Moggers walked inside and saw rows and rows of books. He wandered through the stacks, trying to find a human to talk to. Finally, he saw a young girl sitting at a table, reading a book. He approached her and said, "Excuse me, miss, do you speak cat?"

The girl was shocked. She had never heard a cat talk before! But Moggers was so charming and funny that she couldn't help but befriend him. They spent the whole day talking and laughing, and before Moggers knew it, it was nighttime.

As Moggers was leaving the library, he heard a loud noise coming from a nearby alley. He walked towards the sound and saw a group of rats gathered around a shiny object. Moggers knew that he had to investigate. He approached the rats and asked them what they were doing.

The rats were surprised to see a talking cat, but they explained that they had found a treasure map and were trying to understand it. Moggers was intrigued. He had never been on a treasure hunt before, and he wanted to join the rats on their adventure.

The rats were hesitant at first, but Moggers was persuasive. He convinced them that he

MOGGERS' SPECIAL TALENT

had the skills and smarts to help them find the treasure—and he promised not to eat them. So, the rats reluctantly agreed to let him come along.

The treasure map led them through the city and into a dark, spooky forest. Moggers was nervous, but he didn't let it show. He kept his cool and used his keen sense of smell to track the scent of the treasure.

They walked for hours, and just as they were about to give up, they saw a glimmering light in the distance. They ran towards it and found a huge chest filled with gold coins and jewels.

Moggers couldn't believe his luck. He had always dreamed of finding treasure, and now he had actually done it. The rats were ecstatic too. They thanked Moggers for his help and offered to split the treasure with him.

Moggers was touched by their generosity, but he declined their offer. He told them that the real treasure was the adventure they had shared together. He said that he had never felt so alive and that he was grateful for their friendship.

The rats were touched by Moggers' words, and they knew that he was right. The treasure was just a bonus. It was the journey that mattered.

MOGGERS' SPECIAL TALENT

TEST YOURSELF

1. Why was Moggers able to talk?

    ○ He ate a magic mouse
    ○ He was born that way
    ○ He was half human

2. Where did Moggers meet his human friend?

    ○ On the street
    ○ In an alleyway
    ○ In a library

3. The rats were surprised to meet a talking cat.

    ○ True
    ○ False

DISCUSSION--WRITE OR SPEAK

1. If you could have one magic power, what would it be?

2. If you went on a treasure hunt, what would you like to find?

3. What is the strangest thing you have seen a cat do?

Answers:
1. He ate a magic mouse.
2. In a library.
3. True.

RHYME'S TIME TO SHINE

Once upon a time, in a small town so quaint,
Lived a smart little cat, named Rhyme, who was no saint.
He could only speak in perfect rhyme,
Which was quite a feat, all the time.

Rhyme's owners loved him, as he was quite a delight,
But his rhyming ways could be quite a sight.
For example, when he wanted some fish,
He'd say, "Oh please, do grant my wish!"

But Rhyme's real talent lay in his poetry,
Which was so good, it was plain to see.
His rhyming words were like music to the ear,
And his poetry would bring the townsfolk near.

One day, a poetry contest was held in town,
And Rhyme decided he'd go and take the crown.
He practiced and rehearsed, day and night,
And he felt that his chances of winning were quite bright.

When the day of the contest finally arrived,
Rhyme stepped up to the stage, feeling quite alive.
He cleared his throat and began to recite,
And the townsfolk were amazed at the sight.

RHYME'S TIME TO SHINE

His rhymes were so perfect, they brought tears to the eyes,
And everyone there was in for a surprise.
When the judges announced the winner that day,
It was Rhyme who took the prize away!

From that day forward, Rhyme was a local celebrity,
And his poetry was always in high demand, you see.
Rhyme's fame spread far and wide,
And soon he was known on every side.

People came from all over to hear him speak,
And they would listen intently, their eyes agleam and cheeks rosy pink.
One day, as Rhyme sat by the window sill,
He heard a small kitten's meows, high-pitched and shrill.

He rushed outside to see what was the matter,
And found a little stray kitten, who was all a-clatter.
Rhyme took the kitten under his wing,
And taught him how to rhyme and sing.

The kitten grew up to be quite the wordsmith too,
And together they wrote poems that were ever so true.
And so, Rhyme and his little protégé,
Rhymed their way through night and day.

They brought joy to all those who heard,
Their rhymes, which flowed like a magic word.
The moral of the story, as it's often said,
Is that even a cat can be a wordsmith, with a clever head!

TEST YOURSELF

1. What was rhyme's biggest talent?

    ○ His poetry
    ○ His singing voice
    ○ His dance skills

2. Why were the people so amazed by Rhyme?

    ○ Because he could dance
    ○ Because he was so handsome
    ○ Because his rhymes were so perfect

3. Rhyme won the poetry competition.

    ○ True
    ○ False

DISCUSSION--WRITE OR SPEAK

1. Can you write a short rhyming poem in English?

2. Do you like to read poetry? Why or why not?

3. What is the best concert or show you have ever seen?

Answers:
1. His poetry.
2. Because his rhymes were so perfect.
3. True.

We hope you enjoyed this book!
We would love to hear from you in a review—it inspires us to write new books for you :)

Visit us at
www.bellanovabooks.com
for more great books, including books in other languages.

If you read this book comfortably, then why not check out our series of animal fact books? They're a fun way to learn and read at the same time at a level that is right for you.

www.ingramcontent.com/pod-product-compliance
Lightning Source LLC
LaVergne TN
LVHW092232110526
838202LV00092B/12